THE HIDDEN TREASURES

OF THE

ANCIENT QABALAH

BY

ELIAS GEWURZ

*"And cherish deep
within thy heart
the memory of
those who have
served as a channel
of light to thy
perplexed soul,
and be thou
grateful to them."*
—From the
Golden Precepts
of Trismegistus.

VOL. I

THE TRANSMUTATION OF PASSION INTO POWER

The substance of chapters one to six inclusive has been read before the Krotona Lodge of the Theosophical Society during May and June, 1915. Chapter eight was given before the Krotona institute during the session of February-March, 1915. While chapter seven was read before the Krotona Lodge on the 19th of January, 1915.

WHAT IS THE QABALAH?

The Qabalah is the Secret Doctrine of the Jews, handed down throughout the ages by the great teachers to their beloved disciples under the solemn vow of secrecy.

In the Twelfth Century, however, the principal text-book of the Qabalah was written down by a very learned Rabbi named Moses de Leon. This book is known as the Zohar, and contains inexhaustible mines of occult knowledge. Priceless treasures of mystic lore are scattered in its volumes, awaiting discovery by the intelligent student. The language of the *Zohar*, however (the Hebrew Chaldaic), known to a very few scholars only, constitutes the main difficulty in the way of those desirous of studying the Qabalah.

The learned assemblies of olden times, in which the great Masters of Israel held forth their doctrines, have been the original sources of the philosophy of these latter days. Modern Occultism, too, is derived from the same quarters, and should the pages of the Holy Qabalah be accessible some day to the English student, he will be astonished and delighted at the wealth of occult truth he will find in them.

The books of the Qabalah are fountains of living waters and at a time of great spiritual need, as the present is, the strength and consolation offered us through its teachings are doubly welcome.

The greater part of my life has been devoted to this study, and the teachings given out in my books are all based upon this ancient wisdom of the Rabbis

ELIAS GEWURZ.

Krotona, Hollywood,
Los Angeles, California,
May, 1915.

Rabbi Eleazar, the beloved disciple of the Heavenly flame (Rabbi Simeon), was pondering over the words of the Psalmist, "And unto the broken in heart the Lord is nigh." "Master," he said, "why should it require the breaking of the heart in order to bring God nearer to us?" "My dear child," replied Rabbi Simeon, "the heart of man is ruled by a multitude of powers; their hold upon it is due to Karmic debts, and every attachment is an obligation of past lives. The ineffable light of the Holy One cannot shine through us until these obligations are discharged. It requires a transparent medium to reflect a flame; dense and opaque bodies do not transmit the light falling on them. It is the shine with the heart of man; when its bonds are broken, God draws nigh unto it."

The Vessel in which Transmutation Takes Place

Our birth is but a sleep and a forgetting,
The soul that rises with us our life's star has had elsewhere its
setting
And cometh from afar
Not in entire forgetfulness
And not in rater nakedness
But trailing clouds of glory do we come from God who is our
Home.
                                                    —Wordsworth.

I.

THE VESSEL IN WHICH TRANSMUTATION TAKES PLACE

Man is fearfully and wonderfully made; he is the meeting point of descending and ascending nature; the arena in which the mighty Gods fight their battles, and principalities and powers strive for mastery over it.

The nature of man is so intricate and complex that even this physical constitution alone has not been exhaustively explored as yet.

There are still chambers within chambers and regions within regions, mysterious and unknown. Now if this is so the physical body, which is plainly visible to our senses and the organs and parts of which can be touched and handled, what about our mental and spiritual natures which are much more subtle and more elusive?

If we lack certainty as regards the body terrestrial, how great must our ignorance be when we approach the celestial vehicles?

And yet we cannot say we are without knowledge regarding our higher nature, and much has been given to this generation for which preceding ages longed and yearned in vain. Knowledge has been flowing into our minds for the last four or five decades which has dispersed both the superstitions of the Dogmatic Churches and the arrogant Dicta of the official scientists. But knowledge, no matter how plentiful and profound, is no remedy for human ills, unless it is accompanied by love and by the desire to apply it to its proper use. On the contrary, of two ill-disposed persons the one who knows most is the more dangerous because as his weapons are sharper, they can do more harm.

And, in fact, it so happened that with the advent of knowledge, its abuse grew apace, and side by side with the good, which it brought into the world, it gave birth to all sorts and conditions of evil.

The great mistake made by the seekers of knowledge, a mistake which proved most fatal to their spiritual welfare, was that they sought knowledge for its own sake. This was bound to result in failure and to frustrate the very object of their search. Man's mission on earth is to attain freedom; lie must be freed from all that binds him to earthly associations. This endeavor is the supreme task of man individually and of humanity collectively. The alchemists of old illustrated this pilgrimage of man towards liberation by their various processes, tinctures, and manipulations. Their vessels, laboratories, metals and transmutations were so many names for the one and the same thing, namely, the illumination of the human soul and her redemption from matter. The well-known saying, "To dissolve and to coagulate" meant nothing but to tear asunder the bonds of passion binding the soul to matter and having dissolved even the most subtle threads of desire and attachment, to turn the life stream upwards and to coagulate it with the pure elements of the Soul. The vessel in which this process takes place is the body of man. This vehicle of manifestation is the crucible in which the pure gold is tried and proven, the alloy and the dross burned away, so that only the sterling substance remains

The human body is the real cross upon which crucifixion takes place. Each Ego chooses its own kind of cross according to its special need. If our body happens to be weak and handicaps us in life's race, it is not a misfortune, a misfortune though it seems.

It may be awkward from a material point of view, but looked at from the higher vistas of the spirit it is invariably a blessing and contains some great lesson of which the Ego is in dire need.

It must therefore be borne in mind that while transmutation takes place, and until it is complete, the vessel, which is the body, must needs suffer from the effects of the process going on within it. If the man has been living a riotous life in the past and then suddenly turns the other way about and wishes to become a saint, he cannot do so in the twinkling of an eye; his various bodies, which as we know are living and knowing organisms, do not at once submit to the change of front on the part of their owner. They feel that they ought to have been consulted about the transaction and they make their grievances known by various pains and aches and discomforts. These are generally the symptoms accompanying the process of transmutation. The laboratories of Nature are conducted on the same principle everywhere. Whether it is the chemist trying to compound a medicine or the alchemist trying to create a new substance, they both base their practices upon the eternal and invariable law of affinity which governs the generation and growth of every thing in the vast realms of manifest nature. A little reflection will convince us of this perfect analogy subsisting between nature and man and will help us so to order our lives as to profit by all the wise provisions which she has made for the welfare of leer creatures in all the kingdoms.

When man first turns his eyes heavenward, praying to be lifted up, the task confronting him is tremendous indeed. The age-long associations of body, mind and soul have to be severed and new affinities have to be established. Looking at these things from outside we say one must exercise "self-control." I wonder whether any one of us realizes the fullness of the glory of that human being who has really overcome. It really amounts to the making of a new creature, one ceasing to be a man and beginning to be a God.

We understand, of course, that the real battle is going on inside the man. What we see on the surface are only moving hands on the dial of a clock; the clockwork is inside. The springs of conduct are hidden from our eyes; the cause of things is beyond our ken. We often believe we know ourselves and our interests, but the real man and his real needs pass our comprehension. In his infinite wisdom, the Supreme Lord has thus ordained it that self-knowledge should come to man by degrees. While his nature is being transformed, the knowledge of Self filters in. Just look at the four kinds of yoga taught by the Eastern sages. They were designed to facilitate this introduction of Self-knowledge into the mind and the establishment of normal relations between the Divine and astro-mental parts of man. Raja Yoga was to purify the lower man, Karma Yoga was to turn his energies into sacrificial work, Gnani Yoga was to refine his manasic vehicles by mental exercises and study, and at last Bhakti Yoga was to unite him to God by love and devotion. To most of us it is not given to tread all the paths at the same time; we are limited by our congenital failings, and heredity and environment are against us, so as some of us enter the Path we usually progress along the lines of least resistance.

If we are of a practical turn of mind we become Karma Yogis, if students, we become Gnanis, if we are strong-willed we subdue our bodily and psychic natures and become Raja Yogis, and if our natures are affectionate and the love element is the strongest then we become Bhaktis. All of these lead to the same goal and at last merge into one another.

He who strives for liberation must finally master all. Yoga like Alchemy requires the whole Man; compromise is out of place in these altitudes, and he, who reserves to himself a little foible or some pet indulgence and thinks it will be all right in spite of all, will find it very expensive indeed, because the ladder will give way and the rung he thought he would skip will prove a pitfall for his feet.

The analogy between Yoga and Alchemy is so perfect and so instructive that one cannot help admiring that wonderful spiritual guidance from on high which leas come down to the founders of both these sciences.

You are aware that Yoga comes from the East, while Alchemy comes from the West. I believe that no great work has ever been accomplished by man on earth without help from those Spirits of just men made perfect, who are always around us like clouds of witnesses to render help wherever needed.

Now the System of Yoga has been taught for centuries in India and the practices of Alchemy have been studied for ages in Europe. Both these schools have had helpers in the higher spheres who inspired their labors. That the teachings of both agree in their essential principles is one more proof of their Divine origin. Now the most salient feature of both Yoga and Alchemy is their agreement as to the vessel in which the operation is to take place. It is the body of man; by body I do not mean the physical vehicle only, but the mental body as well. Both have to be put in the furnace and purged from their old dross until the glorified spirit is free. "To produce gold one must have gold" is a Hermetic saying; well, the gold is the spiritual soul within us. It is she who has to be resurrected from the ashes of Self sense and sin so that she may enter into her rightful possessions of the Divine Gifts of virtue, wisdom, and love promised to her by the Giver of all good gifts, the Father of Lights from whom she comes. "Life itself," says Patanjali, "is the great teacher of Yoga." The cosmic procession of life passing before our eyes is the High School par excellence in which the children of men graduate into Yogis of various degrees and rank. Every cycle pushes humanity a little further upon the high road of evolution, and as one spiral is passed and another reached, Man finds he has grown almost imperceptibly in all the graces and accomplishments incidental to the latest stage of unfoldment.

Those who wish to go ahead of their brethren must not wait for the generality of men; they must step out of the beaten track and—as it were—take a hand in their own making. The present moment is very favorable for this independent departure, because the cyclic law favors it and the new dispensation into which we are entering makes it easier of accomplishment. In the mineral, vegetable, and animal kingdoms, the units undergoing evolution are helplessly subject to the law governing the group-soul; on the human plane only does independent initiative come in.

Arrived at this stage the Jiva-Atma or the Spiritual Soul is at liberty to break loose from the mass and to start on its way back to the source of its origin. This way of return is through the chamber of ordeals, the crucible in which transmutation takes place. All metals must be purified and transformed into gold, which means that all outgoing tendencies must he mastered, drawn in, and turned upward so that they may serve to energize the pure Spirit—and help to manifest him according to his dictates instead of drawing him as hitherto after their own inclinations.

It is impossible to describe the process in particular as, owing to Karmic bonds, we all have different burdens to bear, but on the whole it is safe to say that at any time in our life we are to be found in just that place and surrounded by just those conditions which, if understood and respected, would invariably help us to fulfill the law and by so doing draw nearer to the goal, namely, the liberation of our souls from the bondage of illusion. But unfortunately we are never quite reconciled to the hard facts of this world and this life, and even the best of us think we are in the wrong place and if it were not for this, that, and the other, we might be better off, and have a better chance to be happy and good. But my dear Brothers and Sisters, it is not so!

We are, as I said, at every moment of our lives, just where we ought to be, and happy the man who can realize this truth in all its wonderful simplicity. The vessel of transmutation into which we have been thrown will never give us up until we are quite ready and well done; let us not oppose the process and thus retard the advent of our freedom.

As you are aware, everything in this world is governed by analogy The law that governs the atom is the same which governs man, and the law that presides over the evolution of man is identical with the law that rules the universe. Bearing this in mind, how significant every act of ours becomes! Often even slight and seemingly unimportant actions of ours may, in their ramifications, generate karmic results of tremendous importance to our fellow-men and to the world.

Especially is this true of people of high spiritual status. They are doubly responsible for their thoughts, words, and deeds, because they create corresponding effects upon the higher planes.

"To him to whom much is given, of him much shall be required"; that is to say, the man of power must be alive to it, that with the acquisition of power he increases his obligations, and the more powerful he grows, the more sacrificing must he be. When the lower elements of our constitution become transmuted and refined, we acquire great powers and many gifts, and the danger arises that we may not adequately appreciate the solemn duties attaching to them. The law of God can never be broken; it is we who break ourselves in violating its eternal decrees.

Having overcome most desires, as we finally do, in the process of transmutation, we must also overcome the greatest of and most subtle of all desires, and that is the desire for power. Power for its own sake is not worth having, and more than that, it often throws the disciple far deeper down into the abyss than bodily self-indulgence. It is the same with spiritual pride—Pride is the sin against the Holy Ghost, which can never be forgiven. Therefore, when undergoing the transformation of our natures in the crucible of life, we ought to see to it that these subtle and poisonous elements are got rid of in the process.

Let us now recapitulate the main points: As soon as man begins to be dissatisfied with his old life and his old habits and learns to appreciate the grave beauties of the higher life, the process of transmutation is started within his constitution. He may not yet actually have done anything to begin the new life, but the mere resolution to do so plants his feet upon the path. Even to see only the futility of the vain, sinful and empty life, means half the battle won. When a definite step is taken and the desires truly renounced, the Karmic effects are mighty and far-reaching. If the aspirant is strong enough to persist in spite of the trials springing up on every side, as he advances on the Path, then the work of transmutation enters the second stage, which is the stage of unification. Before this is reached, all passion, whether physical or mental, must be rooted out of his nature. Unification is the crown of the great work; it is the reward of ages of effort and æons of hard labor. Truly blessed is the man in whom the Divine Self has been united permanently to the astro-mental part which is all we see of one another while on earth. When this conjunction has taken place, man has ceased to be subject to the laws of man; for him, we have been told, "no law can be framed"; he has ceased to be a child of earth, for he has become in the truest and deepest sense, a child of God.

Now there is one thought I would like to impress strongly upon our minds at this point. It is this: while this higher and nobler life is eminently desirable and all of us would fain attain unto it, we must not forget the grim reality of this every day existence of ours arid, while reaching out for the higher life, let us not by some careless act or acts wreck this prosaic foundation upon which the poetical structure of the life beautiful is to be raised.

Many have made this mistake and destroyed themselves body, mind, and estate, in order to develop spiritually. What they really did achieve was entire ruin both physical and spiritual. Let us in our endeavor to live the higher life be as practical as we are in the management of our mundane affairs. Above all, let us be guided by reason and let us discard everything that is cloudy and vague, and after having done all we possibly can do to guard against the blind forces of the lower nature and to master all that is beneath us, let us remember that we are infinitesimal expressions of the one great law, and we can do nothing better than commend ourselves to its Supreme Author, the great Law-giver. He knows us better than we know ourselves and He loves us better too.

And therefore we say unto this last, "Into Thy hands do we commit our Spirit and our souls into Thy keeping."

The Feminine Elements in Man and their Redeeming Power

Much shall be forgiven unto her who loveth much.

....

....

Love on, through doubt and darkness, and believe
There is no thing which love may not achieve.
—E.W.W.

II.

THE FEMININE ELEMENTS IN MAN AND THEIR REDEEMING POWER

Strength and beauty are the two attractive elements of our nature, but the masculine strength and the feminine beauty are in reality one and the same thing. That which we admire as strength in the man is the same element that fascinates us as beauty in the woman.

The difference consists in the way of their manifestation only. When the spirit has gained sufficient power on the outgoing path and is strong enough to hold the power that is his in eternal potentiality, then beauty appears on the scene and transforms the aggressive forcefulness of the man into the gentle attractiveness of the woman.

To be quite exact, beauty is strength on a higher spiral; when strength ripens, it becomes beauty. This is the spiritual aspect of it, that seems to have been voiced by all the sages of antiquity.

Even savage man of prehistoric times was subject to the attractions of the physically much weaker female, thereby acknowledging her superiority over his brute force.

The law which governs the generation of energy on the inner planes of being also presides over the evolution of beautiful forms; the source whence strength springs is identical with the origin of all that is pleasing to our sight.

Man is by nature the aggressor, the moving factor, whose energy makes the plasticity of the world-soul yield her latent treasures.

Woman, on the other hand, contains these treasures. She is identical with the World-Soul, and in her the strength of man becomes transformed into beauty, which is the higher aspect of strength. Right here I must remind you that in every man is concealed the womanly element just as every woman has masculine qualities. In fact there are such things as womanly men and manly women. Here we are concerned with the spiritual nature, and as regards this, it is well for us to bear in mind that the feminine nature is far superior to the masculine both in its sensitivity to the unseen, and in its capacity of sacrifice and devotion to the ideal.

I do not wish to be understood as depreciating "the mere man." I could not very well do that, but what I want to emphasize is this, that true greatness and nobility of soul are due to those qualities within us which are feminine by nature.

It matters not whether the physical body one wears is that of a male or a female; It is the perfection of the spiritual nature that counts.

Before man can be redeemed his nature must become feminine. Man stands for positive action, while woman is the symbol of passivity. The idea of power is generally associated with active energy, but it requires a stronger will to refrain from action that to act. Therefore is woman's sphere above that of man, and her kingdom must come before man realizes his true nature.

The dissecting and analytical function of the mind is of a masculine character, while the synthesis, the gathering up and consummating, is altogether womanly. This applies to all the realms of nature; to everything under the sun. In the battle of life, while making his pilgrimage through this wilderness of earthly existence, man is like a strong oak, or a trusty, sturdy oaken stem, but woman like a vine clinging in grace and beauty to him.

This expression of female tenderness on the physical plane is only an emblem of the true relation on the plane of spirit. There the companionship is free from the vicissitudes of earth, and partakes of the Divine nature only. The relations between the sexes on the higher planes are in accordance with the heavenly law governing those planes. Those whose good fortune it was to know the pure friendship of a woman on the earth plane have had, even in this life, a foretaste of the Heavenly condition. Its effect upon the physical nature is the same as when the sun draws up the muddy water of a stagnant pool by the roadside, and, changing its vibrations, returns it as the gentle life-giving rain, softening the dry earth.

Thus is the effect of the sweetness and light emanating from a pure soul in whom passion has been stilled and desire transmuted.

It is through this recognition of the spiritual elements within us which are of a feminine nature that the atoms, molecules and particles of the physical body become glorified and healed and the mind becomes illuminated.

The human soul is in possession of the greatest of all Divine gifts—the power to heal other souls; mark you—not only bodies, but Souls.

The gift of healing is in itself a great boon to mankind, but, when to it is added the power to heal the heavy-laden soul of man then the possessor thereof is indeed a favored mortal whom the Gods delight to honor. This spiritual gift of healing can only be exercised by that man or by that woman in whom the mind has been dualized, that is to say, it has become male-female in one. In those in whom this process of mind-dualization has been effected, a new life springs up which, compared to the old one, is like light unto darkness. It is here, right here that the redeeming power of the feminine elements in man is seen. At the first birth man is endowed with the earthly mind, but at the second birth he receives the heavenly one. To the twice-born sons and daughters of God all things are possible.

To some of us this exalted state may seem a dream, but dreams and longings are founded upon true being for no one can long for that which has no existence or the possibility of existence. Perception of coming things is only possible through conception. The physical life we live and all the desires of the flesh that appertain to it are like the sacred lotus of Oriental lands. The root of this lotus is buried in mud and slime, but from this lowly condition it rises through the currents of the river until at last it reaches the air. Here the plant blossoms forth in luxuriant purity, a type and symbol of the highest spiritual development.

Thus it is with sex life. Sex life has its roots in the mud of material life; it rises through the flowing waters of mentality and finally blossoms in the clear air of our spiritual nature, pure, sacred, divine.

Those whose feet have climbed the rugged steeps of the spiritual heights and who have at last reached the summit will understand the need of their trials, and the wisdom which ordained them. It is at the very top of the mountain that the spiritual consciousness opens and man becomes aware of his dual nature. Then, when this highest part of his constitution is mature, he can draw unto himself from surrounding nature that which corresponds to this highest and most potent part in himself.

If he has the Gold (Love) within him, he can draw the very highest from the vast expanse of space by virtue of the law of affinity which makes like attract like.

There is a fundamental difference between the atomic elements of the masculine and feminine principles in nature and this causes the difference in the external form of male and female.

It is a peculiarity of atoms well known to chemists that their behavior depends upon their arrangement, though their nature is not changed. Thus the difference in the constitution between a molecule of ozone and a molecule of oxygen is quite imperceptible, but their properties differ widely. Why this should be so is a mystery which is perfectly unfathomable to physical science. The key to this mystery is to be found elsewhere; it lies in the spiritual forces governing nature from within. The power that determines the mode of life and activity of an atom, or a molecule, is beyond the reach of the microscope and the scalpel; it is a spiritual power which acts in accordance with laws not yet known to the scientific world. These laws are as beneficent as they are wise, and they invariably make for human well-being. Now if we ascend the scale of creation and examine the workings of these atomic arrangements on the higher planes we find the same law holds good and that duality of sex and its effects upon the life of the human species is just as much a mystery as it is on the lower planes. You often hear of the new mental type which is emerging from the present one; this new type is to be a dualized mind. The holy Qabalah teaches that every thought and emotion is represented structurally in invisible substance, the highest and purest aspirations and emotions consist atomically of bisexual human beings dualized in their mental nature and patterned after the shape of primal man. These forces, however, can only operate through those mortals who are struggling to regain their lost condition of pristine purity by long preparations, severe moral discipline and self-denial. Those who have given themselves to the service of humanity, consecrating their life, thought and substance to the furtherance of God's Kingdom and the doing of God's will on earth, will find that all their old passions and desires, having once been transmuted, will now spring up as powers for good within them. Eliphas Levi, the great Qabalist, left his testimony to this effect. The strength of his devotion to the light he had keen, he assured his pupils, was in exact ratio to the strength of his former passions, a force of which he had by severe discipline subdued and turned into a servant of the God within.

All desire is centrifugal, outgoing, while will, pure spiritual will, is centripetal and attractive. Thus do the feminine qualities in our constitution exercise a redeeming power over our old Adamic nature, and, until man understands this bi-une arrangement of his internal make-up, and, understanding it, strives to awaken and deepen the Divine Consciousness within himself so as to become continually and increasingly aware of his duality, there is little chance of his transcending the level of ordinary humanity. But, when this miracle has happened and the eyes of the soul have been opened and the torch of faith has been lit, then man becomes more than man; he has established his right to be a ruler of man.

Christ, the everlasting symbol of all that is true and good and really great, was of a feminine nature. He only wore the body of a man, but His soul was womanly. His life, His labors, His final sacrifice were just the means to fill the measure before His departure from the valley of tears, in which He was to learn all lessons and to suffer all manner of pain, in order that He might be able to help those whose lot in life it was to suffer and to endure. If we wish to benefit by the redeeming power of the feminine elements within us, let us recall the memory of the Lord of Compassion and the agonies of His spiritual crucifixion. It is an ordeal we all must pass through, sooner or later. Let it be sooner.

The supreme message of this ordeal to us is that we may not try to escape from our Karma, but whatever betide us, we should say: "Let this cup pass from me, yet not my will, but *thine* be done." Thus shall we learn to be patient under tribulation and strong in the day of trial.

Millions of human beings, our brothers and sisters, are waiting for our help. We cannot help them until we have ourselves overcome. The physician must first heal himself if he is to be of any use to the patient. It is a hard path to tread, the path of overcoming; it has been called the path of woe, but it is also the path of glory. When we some day arrive at the end of it, we shall understand the words of the Conquering Christ ringing down through the ages—"*It is finished*"—"Consumatum est," as the Latin Bible has it. Yes, then, we too shall say "It is finished"; we have fulfilled the cycle of our destiny. Whenever this comes to pass, our sole concern in this life and the things of this life will only be so far as they relate to the spirit's welfare. Henceforth all our striving, if we strive at all, will be, that, as the days pass by, we may grow juster and fairer and purer, more kind and more true, more silent and more humble, and having attained ourselves, to point out the way to the younger souls corning after us. It is the only means we have to repay the blessed Masters for Their sacrifices, which alone have made our lives worth living.

THE HOLY SUPPER

The Holy Supper is kept, indeed,
Whenever we share another's need.
Not what we give, but what we share,
The gift without the giver is bare.
He who giveth Himself with his gift, feedeth three,
Himself, his needy neighbor, and Me.

Spiritual Companionship Between Man and Woman

What matter if I stand alone?
I wait with joy the coming years;
My heart shall reap where it has sown,
And garner up its fruit of tears.
The stars come nightly to the sky;
The tidal wave unto the sea;
Nor time nor space nor deep nor High
Can keep my own away from me.
—Burroughs.

III.

SPIRITUAL COMPANIONSHIP BETWEEN MAN AND WOMAN

In the ancient temples of Egypt and Chaldea they used to tell the neophyte that whenever he met some truly congenial companion during his subsequent career, it would he a sign that the time of his probation was nearing to the end and that he was soon to be recognized and accepted as a disciple of a great Master. As a rule, those who enter upon the path must dwell alone; solitude and loneliness are their lot. It is only when they have learned to stand alone and to remain unshaken that they are allowed the companionship of a friend. The social life of a man distracts the soul and makes it depend upon the whirl and change of events for its sustenance. When the soul is to awaken to its new and true life, these kaleidoscopic changes must give way to constancy and unity. This cannot be the case until man has been tried and proven in the furnace of affliction. When he has tasted of the bitterness of life's cup and emptied it to the very dregs, when one after the other of what we call life's joys have been taken from him and he has lost his health, his possessions and his friends too, then a sense of utter loneliness comes upon him and he enters what the mystics call the great void. Here he has to stand his trial. If he passes it successfully, he is admitted into the inner court of the temple, and permitted to know the true character of his Karma and the laws under which it operates.

Ordinarily the children of men are ignorant of Karmic law, and they do not know the ways and the means by which they are judged. But the disciple does know these things and this knowledge enables him to work with the law consciously and intelligently. As soon as he can do that, Karma relaxes its rigidity and, instead of the measure of judgment, the Lords of Karma grant him the measure of mercy. That is to say, he can now partake of the things of this world and be in it, without being of it.

Spiritual companionship is one of the blessings that come into the disciple's life at this period. He begins to recover his friends, but this time they are friends of the soul and hound unto him by ties of spiritual affinity. What a comfort and a joy to the suffering soul when she finds a sister soul here on earth in whose company she can make her pilgrimage to the other shore! Blessed are the souls that do find one another while on their journey homeward bound. The help they can render each other covers many planes; the various forces human beings are possessed of, magnetic, electric, sympathetic, mental, psychic and moral are all capable of being raised to higher planes of activity. They are all biological in their essence, and, as such subject to the dominance of the spiritual will.

The union of two beings strengthens the dominion of the will, and especially is this the case if the union is between members of the opposite sex. The reason for this is the difference in the magnetisms of the male and female bodies. Every atom in our constitution is surrounded by a magnetic circle. This magnetic circle consists of positive and negative particles, balancing each other. The mental and spiritual particles of our higher bodies are likewise constituted. Between two human beings of the opposite sex—provided their mentalities are congenial—the same relation exists on a larger scale. The electric elements preponderating in the male organism are balanced by the magnetic currents of the female body acid the harmonious exchange of the magnetisms thus generated is the cause of that feeling of exhilaration and joy which a pure companionship between man and woman invariably produces. So much so, that it often seems that the physical bodies have no weight, but appear to float along without effort. No wonder that the participants in such a union looked forward with great delight to the time when they would meet. The old-fashioned conception of life, the prudery and restraint in the social intercourse of men and women, were responsible for a great deal of harm. Untold misery was the result of most of the marriage-relationships, because the partners did not know each other sufficiently. But apart from it, the most innocent contact between the sexes was looked upon askance by people whose minds have not been pure enough to think of love as a Divine gift that can be expressed on many planes much higher than the physical. Happily, these notions are gradually passing away and man and woman can sustain friendly relations to each other. The evil-minded person, who thinks of wrong at the sight of what is God's most perfect gift to the children of men, that person condemns himself because the evil he sees is in his own mind only. "To the pure all things are pure." To return to our subject, the magnetisms streaming out from the auras of man and woman are differently constituted. Through their interblending, positive and negative life-elements are obtained. This interblending creates life, and life is not a material substance, but a spiritual element, highly refined and potential with great possibilities and with great power.

Now all these benefits to be derived from the association between man and woman are non-existent for those who have not yet mastered their passions and lower emotions. People who live on the lower planes of life may derive a certain pleasure according to their evolutionary status, but this is not what we are here concerned with. The aspirant striving to enter the temple of knowledge and wishing to taste of the heavenly joys of pure and undefiled love must have subdued his desire nature; his mind must be like a limpid lake, calm and tranquil, on the surface of which not a ripple is to be seen.

Having accomplished this purification, man and woman are fit to be spiritual companions, but not otherwise. That it is worth while to go through this ordeal has been testified to by all who have attained unto the goal. There is a love which few have known. It is the love that opens the soul's inner portals and admits our spirit into the holy of holies, the sanctuary of the pure soul. There the glory of the Divine image is restored, and nature crowns the victor with the laurels of a consummate happiness, of which in ordinary life there is naught to serve us as an illustration.

Wisdom, the ultimate aim of life, can only be acquired if the law leas been fulfilled. The fulfillment of the law implies that we have had our share of all experiences—if some of them are missed our education is incomplete. Before we attain unto final liberation we must ascend the ladder of earthly life and view from every rung of it the world around us. It is this which is meant when we are told "to look intelligently into the heart of men." We must learn our own lessons, even the highest, by passing through the full gamut of the things which human life has to offer. There are, however, two ways of passing it—the lawful one and the lawless one.

The lawful way of gaining experience on earth is the partaking of all it has to offer under the guidance of the Spirit and only in proportion to the Spirit's actual needs. Lawlessness steps in when we desire for the sake of desire and do not respect the Soul's protestations. The disciple to whom desire is only a means of gaining knowledge uses it in accordance with the eternal design which called it forth. On whatever plane desire exists, it is only a means to an end for him and he does not allow it to tarnish his higher nature, or to create within him the germ of attachment to any form or shape of it. This resignation in the midst of the objects of desire is productive of great and lasting strength. The continual balancing of the centrifugal and centripetal forces of spirit generates the Divine power of overcoming all the ailments of body and soul and endows us with the supreme virtue of healing all manner of disease.

The spiritual companionship between man and woman has the acquisition of this power for its purpose. Owing to her experience in past lives, woman's interior nature is more centered in love than man's and consequently she supplies the necessary welding power to hold man's psychical and spiritual natures to a given centre. The Divine self though ever present in both sexes cannot appear to us, unless the love and power elements are blended and eternal silence has been borne in the soul.

As man and woman grow in spiritual worth, their power and influence for good go on increasing and they become focal points for the hosts of heaven watching over humanity. Under the guidance of these guardians, and, while doing their bidding and cultivating their higher nature, man and woman grow in all excellence.

Those treading the path of discipleship find great help in such a congenial companionship. The continuous transmutation of bodily structure is attained and furthered through such soul communion; and through the mental activity consequent upon it, the body is changed cell by cell. This transmutation is the same as the alchemic process by which food and drink and breath are changed into blood, from blood into aerial fluid and then into etheric or mental substance. Then the ego touches it by its own vibrations and it becomes more etherealized into soul or auraic essence.

Every conscious effort we make to uplift and refine the physical body is a step towards the quickening of our spiritual faculties, the deepening of our insight and the increase in wisdom and understanding. The process of life is a continuous chain of sublimation and refinement.

Beginning with the lowest and crudest forms of matter right up to the highest expression of life, everything is undergoing evolution and transformation. Speaking of matter, we are thinking of tangible material such as we can see or touch or recognize by the physical senses, but air is matter and we live completely immersed in it and in other airs, that is to say, finer elements than the one we call air. In these tenuous regions our evolution is going on while we are unaware of it. But all the same is the substance of those planes subject to the universal law of transmutation. We are, as it were, unconscious agents of nature on those planes, and she uses us to effect her designs everywhere.

The higher virtues of love and devotion subserve this purpose of refinement on the higher planes. You often heard it stated by our great teachers that the sentiment of love purifies the emotional body; so does the sentiment of devotion. It virtually then comes to it that, even when we think that we are acting in a most spontaneous way, bestowing our love upon the object of our affection, or offering our devotion to our ideal, even then we are only instruments of nature who works through us like a clever craftsman in the execution of his plans.

At the same time, we must bear in mind that when we are used as agents on those higher planes, it is well with us because we are then free from the lower forms of Karma to which those on the material plane of life are still subject. This is one of the benefits of spiritual companionship; it advances us by planting within us the seeds of love and veneration and turning the emotional and passional forces of our nature towards the inmost and the highest, thus giving us a foretaste of the pure and selfless Divine love which we shall some day realize on the higher ranges of cosmic life.

To conclude, let us review the main benefits derivable from the association of man and woman in a pure spiritual companionship. First, the relation must be established between people of congenial natures; they must love the same things and be devoted to the same ideal; the more such ideals they have in common, the better for them, for their ties are strengthened thereby.

Second in importance, but not to be underestimated, is the physical constitution of those associating. Some people think they can slight this aspect but it is not so. Though true sympathy is of an interior nature, it must not be forgotten that our senses are avenues to the spirit and things that are to commend themselves to the Spirit must be pleasing and acceptable to its sentinels outside, which we call our senses.

Perfect sympathy can only subsist between partners whose bodily constitutions only introduce true harmony into their relationship. Where the slightest repulsion exists, owing to external antipathy, the bond of union must needs be weakened. If harmony has been established on the physical, mental and spiritual planes, and the purpose of the given association is to serve the highest which both partners cognize, then Divine revelation comes to them and enlightens them in all things. It is the Voice of God in the garden telling how to crown the sanctified life with beauty and joy and how to make it a milestone for the wayfarers of succeeding generations.

Star to star vibrates light, why not soul to soul? If the purpose of life is beneficent, as we know it is, is it not the duty of each being to serve as a channel for the spread of light and the increase of joy? When two human beings are united for this object on earth, the angelic hosts on high bless their union and take them into their charge. They are led through the highways and byways of life and shown the untold misery and suffering calling for aid and comfort. Looking round them, they learn how to love those who know not what love is, how to pity, how to help and how to grow God-like. Thus strengthened by their own devotion to each other, they pass along on their mission of mercy, pouring out their benedictions upon the needy and distressed with whom their Karma brings them in contact. Their own pure personal love has taught them love Divine which is purer still.

Having profited by their association in body, mind and soul, they now work on the plane of spirit, as servants of the most high God. Truly blessed is the portion of such, for they have found favor above all other mortals, and, even when all things of earth shall pass away, their loving deeds will live. For such there is no fear of death, for, having fulfilled the cycle of their destiny on earth, they will continue their labors of love in the regions beyond, in the gracious presence of the Lord of Hosts, of whom we are told that "His mercies endure forever and his compassions never fail."

A picket frozen on his duty,
A mother starved for her brood,
Socrates drinking the Hemlock,
And Jesus on the Rood.
And the millions who, humble and nameless,
The narrow pathway of duty have trod;
Some call it consecration,
While others call it God.

IV.

THE KNOWLEDGE OF GOD OBTAINABLE THROUGH LOVE PURE AND UNDEFILED

The vague notions still prevailing among leaders of thought as to what constitutes the summum bonum, the highest happiness, are responsible for most of the chaos of our social life and our systems of education. As long as we are not quite certain as to what the goal of humanity really is, we cannot possibly order our lives to the best advantage. Man's chief glory is the faculty whereby he knows. As long as material conditions constrain him to spend the greater part of his life in manual labor, he cannot of course devote much time to the cultivation of his intellect; but, since the advent of scientific devices for labor-saving, humanity has been in a better position to care for the intellectual upliftment of the masses. The Higher Education has been increasing, art and literature are flourishing and every one, no matter how humble he be, seems to be anxious for knowledge and eager for culture. With the progress of the sciences, however, the problem arose how to utilize their application so that it might result in the greatest happiness for the greatest number. This is indeed a mighty problem, worthy of the attention of the best and bravest of men. How can we use these God-given gifts of inventors and their discoveries, so that they may not result in multiplying human misery but rather in its reduction and final elimination? The answer has not yet been found so far as practical life is concerned. We still use our best energies and the most clever intellects to manufacture implements of war and to organize bodies of men against one another. Our economical conditions too are in a state of perpetual disorder. Each man is for himself; millions are perishing annually for lack of the very necessaries of life, and few of us seem to care. There is plenty of food and an abundance of everything to make life comfortable, but the good will seems to be lacking to make all these good things subserve their proper purpose, namely, the welfare of all.

As man masters nature and frees himself from her tyranny, the need for utilizing all her forces to increase the sum total of human happiness dawns upon him. He realizes the vanity of all things which narrow his horizon and the poverty of even the greatest of pleasures if they serve only the petty self. In this age and generation, the waves of social sympathy rise very high and, amidst the indifference of the rich and mighty ones, many a man says to himself, "I am my brother's keeper; his troubles are mine, and I am responsible for his wellbeing." The public institutions we possess, all the social arrangements for the welfare of the poor and helpless ones, who have fallen by the wayside, are due to the efforts of those chosen ones who have realized the seriousness of life, and, wishing to make the best of it, are devoting their possessions and their energies to ameliorate the conditions of the oppressed and downtrodden ones so as to bring a little of the sweetness and light of civilization into the aching hearts of the eternally disinherited. But man does not live by bread alone, and his need of spiritual and intellectual sustenance is just as great and as pressing as that of physical nourishment. The strongest desire of man is to know. He wants to know the world in which he lives, the body he calls his own, the soul he believes inspires him and the God from whom she comes. All these things man wants to know, and the more time advances towards the end of the cycle, the greater grows his eagerness for that knowledge.

After securing the comforts of life and ease and leisure, man hungers for mental and spiritual satisfaction. Of all the defects of the present organization of society and of the cruelties consequent upon it, none is so fatal to the welfare of man as the denial of knowledge to the enquiring mind and of the chance of culture to the aspiring soul. The absence of these opportunities is the most blighting factor of the competitive system, because it deprives man of his natural and legitimate right to acquire all the knowledge he can about himself and his environment. The greatest privileges of man being his capacity to know, anything that denies to him the exercise of this faculty is an unmitigated evil. But it is not only knowledge of material things which the mind craves; the desire to know comprehends things unseen as well. The soul of man yearns for nothing more deeply than for the knowledge of God. The vistas of knowledge are infinite, but not even the highest can satisfy the heart of man. It is only in the knowledge of God that man can find lasting peace. "It is possible to know God," says an occult writer, but it is not easy to acquire that knowledge. The Rosicrucians used to say, "In order to know God one must be God," which means that we must transcend ourselves altogether, and reach out to the sublime heights of the Eternal. Unknown to the indifferent and slothful, God reveals himself to the searching heart and rewards its persistent labors and earnest seeking by the supreme gift of the knowledge of Himself.

"To know God is life eternal," says the apostle; the two are identical. For in ordinary life our perspective is limited to this mundane plane, and we can only know by means of the lower mind, but, when our intuition takes the place of reason, and illumination that of speculation, we know, even as we are known.

Here is a Heavenly promise to man: "Those who seek me, shall find me, if they seek me with all their heart and all their soul." The trend of modern life is towards the spiritual side of things. Science and philosophy are both engaged in paving the way to a more intimate acquaintance with things spiritual. Man as a unit, and as a member of the collective body of the human race, seeks for God in everything he does, but he does not always seek Him rightly, which is the reason of his partial success; but the tendency of human endeavor is growing more and more towards the spiritual. In all departments of life men begin to realize the need for a readjustment of values and for the subordination of the material side of life to the ideal one. This leads to numerous improvements in the methods of labor and to social reconstruction.

The love of God, being the crown of the inner life, is thus expressed in practical life in the service of man. That passion, which formerly made for acquisition, is now under the influence of growing knowledge transmuted into the passion for doing good.

Ambition having fulfilled its purpose in former cycles, when infant humanity wanted it as a spur to exertion and action, is now stepping into the background and her place is taken by man's desire to serve and to be useful. "God's own synonym is use," says a wise proverb, and, as we were made in the image and likeness of God, it behooves us, also, to be of use; only thus do we grow Godlike.

The knowledge of God is best acquired by the practical expression of the Divine attributes in actual life. It is the loving service we render wherever it is called for, which endows us with these attributes. Love, pure and undefiled, expressed in practical every-day life is God's own activity performed by His deputies in human form on earth.

There are two paths of union with God, according to the mystics of old; the path of Knowledge and the path of Love. Those who unite themselves to God by knowledge will sooner or later see the need of love to strengthen the bond of union, while those whose lives are full of devotion must supplement their endeavors by searching and seeking after the deeper mysteries of God-hood revealed by knowledge. The ancient Sages, the great Masters of the Inner Wisdom, taught that the knowledge of God, when obtained, makes of mortal man an immortal. The pure love which helped the acquisition of that knowledge while the disciple was treading the Path, provides him with his glorious garments when he arrives at his destination. These garments are woven of good deeds done, and of noble causes helped during the earthly life; on the heavenly planes their memory becomes the germinating seed for deeds of mercy to be done in future lives. The path of beauty and joy, the path of peace and bliss, converge at the same point. From all sides do the wanderers arrive, but the object of their pilgrimage is the same. It is the temple of wisdom from whence light streameth out in all directions. Humanity has to battle through the iron age with all the horrors incidental to it, before man attains unto his spiritual consciousness. While the battle lasts, every effort counts and every single step taken by the individual pioneers brings mankind nearer to the portals of the sanctuary in which all mysteries will be solved and all tears will be dried. There man will learn to understand the secret of his voyage through the cycles of time, and the purpose of his sojourn on earth. Until that time arrives all our work is only preparatory.

To utilize the fleeting moments, to obey the Spirits' guidance, to detach ourselves from all that drags us down and to join forces with all that lifts us upward, that is our task for the present. The knowledge of God is obtainable and will be ours, but the only way we can attain unto it is by the constant practice of charity in thought, word and deed, and by the expression of love pure and undefiled.

O, sometimes comes to soul and sense
The feeling which is evidence
That very near about us lies
The realm of Spirit mysteries.—*Whittier.*

V.

THE MYSTERY OF TIME AND SPACE

Time and space are the fundamental conceptions which form the warp and woof of our thought. We cannot think of anything except it is, was or is to be, and yet, in their very essence, time and space are the most elusive of problems and can never be grasped by the mind of man. What is time? What is space? What existed before time began, and what will remain when time is no more? What does space mean? Is it a homogenous substance of one kind? or is it heterogeneous and formed of a variety of elements? Where does space cease to be? What is there where space is not? Now these are a few questions very interesting indeed and pregnant with thought. We may not succeed in finding a final solution to the lot of them, but we may perchance succeed in contributing a mite towards a better understanding of them.

Science, the interpreter of the laws of nature and of the principles underlying them, cannot help us in our search to solve the mystery of time and space. The proper domain of Science is the physical universe.

This modern archangel (science) has no wings. An invincible giant, when her feet touch the earth, her marvelous power, her initiative, wisdom and penetrating intelligence are all gone the moment she rises above the soil, and, though it be only a few inches, upon this battlefield she is overcome at once—faint and almost inanimate in an unequal battle because she could not readjust her energies to new conditions. At present science is a child of earth and waits for her redeemer, through whom she will be born again a child from heaven.

In the matter of positive investigations, science has no equal; she is almost infallible, but she is at once rendered powerless when confronted by a problem of the spiritual order, or even when it concerns a—so to say—mixed problem (such as the genesis of matter or the abnormal organic growths of animals or plants) science is silent, or perhaps just stammers.

Now that which the seemingly almighty scientific mind cannot accomplish by its own unaided efforts, the spiritually awakened soul can, and often does, accomplish. Time and space do not exist for the soul of man. The mystery which they constitute to the earthly mind is non-existent to the enlightened spirit. Time, or the succession of events pertain to things material. On the spiritual planes we live in feeling and thought, and it is the feebleness or strength of these which determines the quality of our life on those planes, and distinguishes one being from another. Space again is equally illusory to the soul. Spirit is not separated from spirit by distance, but by discord of nature, and on the other hand spirit is not united to spirit except by the affinity subsisting between them. We can be thousands of miles away from our loved ones but we do not get estranged from them thereby, whereas we may be very close in space to one wishing us ill, and the fact of spatial proximity will not bring our souls nearer to each other. The eternity of time and the infinity of space can be viewed and grasped by those beings only whose minds have learned to function beyond those concepts. Just like the law of Karma which must be transcended in order to be understood, so must the limits of time and space be got rid of by the spiritualization of our thought before we can grasp their meaning. To incarnate humanity, dependent in a thousand different ways upon material conditions, time and space are necessary conceptions; without them there would be chaos in our minds. But for the liberated soul, even on the earth plane, time and space can be relegated to the limbo of things superfluous.

When man once makes up his mind to live the higher life and to think of every experience as related to the spirit and either helpful or hurtful to it, then time and space will matter little to him. His motive and his action and the spirit that prompts them are all that he cares for, from the moment of his surrender.

The dignity and meaning of our lives do not depend upon the years we have lived, nor does the height of our spiritual stature hear any relation to our physical dimension in space. It is only the things which make for growth in perfection that really do count.

And, on the other hand, only those events injure us which weaken our faith and obscure the larger hope. The education and spiritualization of our will being the immediate object of our terrestial existence, time and space signify to us only as much as they serve that object. The only other purpose which time and space serve is the lessening of the evils inherent in the lower life of the race.

The evils from which humanity suffers are not eternal, but confined io the limits of time. They diminish and their intensity decreases in the same proportion as humanity expands its life both in space and in time. The end of all those evils will be their ultimate disappearance by being reduced to what geometry call the "infinitely little." It will happen in the same way—to use a simple illustration—as would be the case if a pound of salt were thrown into a bucketful of water; it would *strongly* salt it, while, if it were thrown into a cistern, it would only *very slightly do so.* In a pond, its taste would hardly be noticeable, and absolutely nothing would remain of its effect if it were thrown into a river. Humanity's evils, too, will disappear in the infinity of space and the eternity of time.

Time and space are the remedies which can cure the evils afflicting mankind. These evils would be incurable had Adam (the universal man, or group soul) preserved its life unchangeably. He had to be divided in space, in order to be healed and for the sake of his reduction and division *ad infinitum* by means of time; whenever this division is accomplished time will come to an end, and divisible space will disappear. Then will Adam (the universal life) return to its primitive state of an indivisible and immortal unity.

Death is only a phenomenal change, and of no more consequence to man than the other changes he has to undergo in the course of his evolution. It simply transmutes the human being from the state of visible nature into that of formless and invisible substance, just like birth manifests what was formerly in a state of substance, on the plans of visible nature.

The old Kabbalists used to express it in a like manner: "There is no birth, nor death, only continual change and transformation from state to state. This makes up the being and existence of all the kingdoms, mineral, vegetable, animal and human."

So time and space fulfill their mission by curing the evils from which mankind must needs suffer in its early stages of evolution and by providing the race with the means of redemption from all that is base and unworthy.

Having freed himself from the limitations of time and space, man realizes that he is a citizen of this grand cosmos and that his rights and privileges, as an immortal and eternally progressive being, cannot be gainsaid. In the infinity of the universe man feels for the first time at home. He never again fears spiritual extinction, for his deathless soul ensures for him life everlasting. If man identifies himself with nature, he has to be transformed by her, if, with the Spirit, he is redeemed by God.

There is no death anywhere, except the unconsciousness of God's presence. To acquire an abiding consciousness of God's presence means to have transcended both time and space, to live in the spirit and to prepare one's self for service in the higher worlds and vaster systems, where there is neither time nor space, but where the Divine Spirit grows in all excellence and perfection.

To the world at large these things sound strange, but to the children of light, whose affections are set on things above, a glimpse comes now and then of the glories awaiting the man who has overcome.

The process of overcoming is an individual one and can only be known by the soul that experiences it. The words of the prophet remain forever true, "and to him that overcometh I will give to eat of the hidden Mannah, and a white stone will I give him, and on it shall be written a new name which no one knoweth save him who receiveth it."

For only they who in full completeness
Have drained life's wine to its very lees,
With all its bitterness and all its sweetness
Can joy completely in God's great peace.
—Hawthorne.

VI.

THE PEACE THAT PASSETH UNDERSTANDING

Saint Augustine was one of those few Church Fathers gifted with the true vision. One of his beautiful sayings is to the effect that "Our hearts shall ever be restless until they find rest in God." In the course of out journey through life we try to assuage our pain by many things. We plunge into work and think that will make us forget the dreariness of our existence, but, failing to find satisfaction in work, we try pleasure, and naturally that, too, is disappointing—even more so. And so again we try mental culture, but with no greater success, and then we despair and begin to wonder whether there are such things as peace and contentment to be found in this valley of tears we call earth. Despair is generally a forerunner of better things, and when a man is good enough to despair of himself, it shows there is still something left in him worth tribulation. This something begins to show its vitality when it alone, of all things, has been left. Tolstoy says that man's worth to the community where he lives and to the world in general, dates from the day on which he knows himself to be worthless—when he loses all, he gains all. To the seekers of peace something similar happens. Peace is a plant which grows in the desert of our inner nature only. When everything has become like a desert, when everything has been dried up, even our tears, when we can no longer cry, and the very flower of life has faded, then Peace germinates in the parched soil of the desolate heart; and, just like the fair flowers in the garden, our lives begin to emanate their sweetest fragrance when we are bruised and wilted and altogether trodden down. This applies to the occult life especially; the occult life—the one we have to live in this world, surrounded by its hardships and cares. Our every relation to people and environment is indicative of our occult status. The circumstances are our teachers and, if we do not learn from them, our life has been lived in vain.

Just look at the rose, and its form and color, the fine lovely texture of its petals and its sweet aroma. It is only because the sweet spirit that animates it knew how to adapt itself to its environment and to attract all that was needful for its growth and perfection, that the rose became what it is. The same law holds good on the human plane. Let us be like the spirit of the rose and we, too, shall dispense the benediction of our qualities to all that pass by. Those who seek peace must vibrate it themselves. But peace cannot be found before its time, for it must be borne in mind that for long periods during our evolution strife and stress are necessary. When, however, the time arrives for the soul of man to rest from her toils, there enters the heart a kind of rhythm which we call peace.

Peace is to the heart what rhythm is to matter; even in the physical organism, a kind of rhythmic peace must obtain. The soul's atoms are mingled with other lower atoms, but never combined. An illustration from chemistry will help us to understand this clearly:

Oxygen in pure air is mixed, but not combined, with nitrogen. When these two gases are combined, according to their proportions, the result is a deadly poison. This is exactly the internal process. When the atoms of the various parts are mingled harmoniously, the result is physical and spiritual well-being; when discord ruptures the rhythm of their vibrations and their harmonious balance, disintegration sets in and disease results.

If matter moves rhythmically, it is pleasing to our eyes, and our feeling on beholding it is a restful one. In the heart of man peace fulfills the same functions. Without it nothing of worth can be accomplished by man; while to the peaceful soul all things are possible.

The mistake modern intellectualism makes is in believing that the brain is the real agent in all important work; the serious observer of life knows this to be a fallacy. The brain is not the important part of the house in which man resides. The centre of life is the heart, and, if consciousness does not take its residence in the centre of life, it will become separate from life and cease to be. Those who desire to develop spiritually must think with their hearts.

Man is a constellation of powers in which all kinds of seeds are contained. The heart is the seat of the central power from which all the others derive their vitality and inspiration. That they may live and function properly, the central power must be at peace with itself and with each one of them. When this is the case, peace reigns supreme and registers itself in the countenance by an attractive angelic radiance. Kindliness and peacefulness always produce beauty and give the face a touch of heaven, for beauty is the light of the soul reflected in the forms of matter.

All of us have at one time or another met people who were a perpetual mystery to us, owing to their constant and changeless calm. Nothing seemed to ruffle them; they took everything just as it happened, and everybody just as he was. They seemed to desire no change and no variation of anything. They were the people who have discovered the secret of peace. As long as "man's inhumanity to man makes countless millions mourn," that peace is beyond attainment for the majority of the race. When the Sun of righteousness arises some day and man realizes the unity of all that lives and breathes, peace will be his. At present it must be won by a prayer of the individual soul, who feels sorely in need of it. There are thousands of such souls everywhere, and to them the message from on High has come down, "Call upon me and I will answer thee, and I will show thee great and mighty things, and I will heal thee and give thee an abundance of truth and peace."

True prayer has a scientific basis; its effect is as certain as that of any other cause in nature. Let us pray for peace and we shall obtain it, even in the midst of stress and storm. When it enters our hearts, we shall know it by the feeling of reconciliation with which it will suffuse our whole being. After that we shall rebel against nothing. For God is enough, and his abiding presence in the soul of man makes her desire naught else.

Thus in the silence which follows the storm the precious jewel is found. At last the harassed soul is at rest and, self-contained, wishes for nothing outside herself. She has found the peace of God, the peace which the world cannot give, neither can it take it away; the peace which passeth all understanding.

And enter not into judgment
with us, for in thy sight no
living man shall be justified.

VII.

JUSTICE AND MERCY

When does one become a Master? When one has learned all the lessons that earth has to teach. How does one learn all these lessons? By submitting to all the experiences natural to this sphere without repulsion when they are painful and without attachment when they seem to be pleasant. Thus, taking things as they are, and letting them all deliver their message, the period of schooling is shortened for the disciple, and his entrance upon the higher stages of the path begins earlier than would have been the case, had he allowed the various qualities of his constitution, called Gunas in the East, to play havoc with his desire nature or to otherwise detain him. There is a saying, "When the disciple is ready, the Master is ready also." When the disciple is ready means that he has arrived at a stage when he can listen to that voice which has bee&. called "the Voice of the Silence," because: we only hear it when we have passed through the silence and accustomed ourselves to live and move and have our being in it.

The first four rules of Light on the Path show us how to pass through the Silence safely. The rule we shall consider tonight is the third. "Before the voice can speak in the presence of the Master it must have lost the power to wound." There is a little story of an old Rabbi, a great teacher of the Qabalah, whose first few words when arising in the morning were, "Heavenly Father, may I during this day and until I again close my eyes in sleep not be made the instrument of judgment against any brother or sister of mine." At first sight it seems as if this is just a common prayer for help from outside, but it is not. Its scientific foundation is the same as the one underlying the precepts in the hall of learning which, as you know, are all truths founded in Nature. In our earlier days, when we used to pray in the old-fashioned manner. the object of our prayers appeared to be to make us good, but later on when we learned to know the true inwardness of things and the purpose of human life, we found that many a thing which sounded as a religious threat was, in reality, a statement of fact inherent in the nature of things. Now, when the Master Hilarion caused to be written down this rule, that "before we can speak in the presence of the Great Ones our voices must lose their power to wound," he did not mean to give us a good bit of advice, with a promise attached to it—that if we are good the Masters will listen to us. No more did the old Rabbi mean anything of this sort. The idea both had in mind is the everlasting truth written in the very heart of the cosmic law. That law determines that on every plane units shall be used for the improvement of their species. We see this law governing the mineral, vegetable and animal kingdoms, but it generally escapes our attention that it also holds good in the human kingdom. Nature in her vast domains uses individuals and entities to further the growth of the collective bodies of which they are the units. Continual progress is nature's aim, and, on the human plane, she achieves it by making every man his brother's keeper. The feeling of repulsion which we experience at a wrong or careless act of a fellow-man is Nature's safeguard against the recurrence of a similar act. She put us where we are in order to eliminate the possibilities of wrong-doing. But now, there are various ways and means of achieving that end. Punishment is one way and instruction is another. On the lower mental level, reaction is so quick and violent that it punishes both the wrong-doer and him who is the witness of wrong-doing, but, on the higher mental level and on the planes beyond it, where the spiritual consciousness is wide-awake, reaction is of a reflective and deliberate character and can select the mode of its response to any form of discordant action. This principle was known to the sages and teachers of the past, but the cycle of evolution did not admit of its universal application. In this century, however, we find it percolating slowly the social conscience, so that even in state-prisons it is found to be better policy to make the confinement of prisoners remedial, rather than vindictive. Now, we as students of the Wisdom-Religion, realize that there must be an exact correspondence of these happenings on the outer plane, within the interior regions of our collective soul life, of which our social structure is but a temporary and transient expression. We see Nature using us individuals as instruments to carry out her behests and while so doing refining both instrument and materials. On the plane on which those we call Masters work, there is no room for violence or for anything like it. Correction there is, by means of loving instruction only. Now, as the Theosophical Society is, so to say, the training-ground for future disciples, those who watch over it find it necessary from time to time to communicate to us some of the rules governing life on those exalted planes. "Light on the Path" is such a communication, and the rule we are now considering is the one destined to regulate the relations between individuals aspiring to follow in the footsteps of those Holy Teachers who have learned all their lessons in past æons of evolution.

Now, apart from the reaction to wrong, which takes actual form by punishment, there is a finer and subtler mode of reaction known as criticism or judgment. To have lost the power to wound, our capacity to criticise and judge must have undergone the same change as the social custom of punishing crime is gradually undergoing. Our very way of looking at things must change. To students of Theosophy this should be easier than to those ignorant of the Ancient Wisdom. We, who know that the personal life is an illusion and that this whole existence is simply Maya, created by Nature in order to evolve the true self, should not find it hard to see that the tendency to wound, whether it be by thought, or word, or deed, is one of the deceptions practiced upon us by external nature, prior to the awakening of our true selves. It is she who makes us resent wrong and repel the wrongdoer. Our True Self knows no resentment and is free from repulsion. In days to come it will be as uncommon to criticise a spiritual failing as it is today to criticise a physical one. Even at the present time, well-brought-up children would not laugh at a blind man, or at a lame one, nor would they make fun of the deaf and dumb; and yet, does it ever occur to us that, whatever the misbehavior, crime or vice of a fellowman may be, if it awakens in us any other feeling than love and pity it is because we are not yet well-brought-up children on the plane of spirit. When the Sixth Root Race arrives there will probably be hospitals for criminals and nursing homes for vicious people, and they will all be treated with the same loving care as we now treat those who are sick in body. It is to prepare us for this stage that "Light on the Path" has been given to us. "Before the voice can speak in the presence of the Masters it must have lost the power to wound." To realize this rule in its fulness means to be free from the tyranny of Nature, and, instead of being unconscious instruments in her hands to chastise and to give pain, we become teachers and helpers and healers, and exercise mercy instead of judgment.

Every time we are called upon to act, we are faced by our trial, and it depends upon our attitude whether the doors to further progress shall be opened to us.

The first of the vestures we have to lay down at the entrance to the temple is that innate tendency to judge and to criticise, because it is a loveless proclivity of the old Adam, and within the temple there is no room for that which is loveless. Therefore the great Masters of the Inner Wisdom warned us that before our voice can be raised in their presence it must have lost the power to wound. As long as it wounds, man cannot teach, neither can he help. Those who wish to become helpers of the race must not be instruments of judgment, and that is why the old Rabbi, the teacher of the Kabala, prayed every morning immediately after rising, "Heavenly Father, may I during this day and until I again close my eyes in sleep, not be made the instrument of judgment against any brother or sister of mine."

I know not where his islands lift
Their fronded palms in air,
I only know I cannot drift
Beyond his love and care.
                         —*Whittier.*

VIII.

ON THE THRESHOLD OF THE SANCTUARY

"Before the soul can stand in the presence of the Master she must have been washed in the blood of the heart." The blood of the heart is, as we know, the life-essence and for the soul to have been washed therein means that life and all that belongs to it of joy and sorrow has been relegated to a secondary place and that the foremost consideration of that soul is now the will of her Lord who has been revealed to her in the process of surrender. It is during this process of bathing in the life-essence that the soul discovers some one, whom alone she would like to serve. During the years of our indiscretion, while we are driven hither and thither by our various likes and dislikes, we serve many Masters, who often prove veritable tyrants to us, but when we have had enough of them, we find that there is a Master of a different stamp, who lives not by our passions and desires, but rather by their suppression and subdual. Now before the soul has made this discovery, it is of no use for her to aspire to the true Masters' presence. In fact, it may harm her to venture thus far. We often find among seekers after truth, persons who have overstrained themselves in one way or another and made themselves physical and mental wrecks in their effort to find and live the higher life. The reason for this is their disregard of the advice given to occultists by all the great and good ones in respect to the dangers of the razor-edged path. You remember how H. P. B., in the

"Voice of Silence," admonishes us to see to it that the ladder does not give way while we ascend its rungs.

The rungs of the ladder on which we climb upward are our weaknesses and bodily failings. To overcome these is our first task before we enter the outer court of the temple. To enter into the Holy of Holies with the old desires clinging to us, spells disaster. No truly-great teacher will accept a pupil who does not seek, by renunciation and by devotion to prove himself worthy of the wisdom which he is striving to attain. In the Gita we are told that no one is to be taught the higher truths who does not practice Tapas, which means renunciation of all that is of the earth earthy. In the Upanishads too, great stress is laid upon self-control, and the great Yogis of the East have at all times been ascetics first and disciples afterwards.

To stand in the presence of the Master implies to he a channel to their sublime teachings, but how can one serve as a channel who has not been purified? You would not think of drinking water that runs through an unclean pipe, for fear of its having been contaminated. No more can one benefit by a spiritual channel which is not thoroughly clean, for fear of the impurities that may have found their way into it during the process of transmission.

The blood of the heart symbolizes the passions of the earthly man, and, in their control and final extinction, lies the secret of regeneration. The Path of Discipleship is strewn with many wrecks on account of the failure to heed the warnings of our ancient teachers who told us of the many pitfalls on the way. The Master Hilarion, who inspired *The Light of the Path* and who occupies a high rank in the great Hierarchy, had probably unique opportunities to study the ways and means that best secure and shorten the passage to the other shore. From his exalted position, he could observe those who succeeded and those who failed and he also saw the reason why. In this gem of occult literature, called *Light of the Path*, he gives us the benefit of his experiences. If we value our higher life we should not neglect so expert an advice as that of Master Hilarion. That which troubles us most in treading the Path is our habit of compromise. We are not whole-hearted and generally do things by halves, the result being that, whenever we enter upon the higher stages of advancement, we find many things to be undone and many a habit to be broken. In those high altitudes the lightest discord creates wrong vibrations which baffle the young soul just emerging from the Egyptian darkness and not only bar her way to further progress but often throw her back into the abyss of repeated incarnations in matter. This is not a figurative mode of illustration, but a statement of actual fact.

There are two passages in The Outer Court to which I would like to call your special attention. Here is the first: "When once a soul has passed through the gateway of the Temple, she goeth out no more." The other passage is a quotation from the Upanishads. It says, "If a man would find his soul, the first thing to do is to cease from evil ways."

Now these two passages are complementary to each other, as you will see presently. First, what does it mean "When a man enters the Temple he goeth out no more." Well, it is this: If we pledge ourselves to service and enter the Path, there can never be any withdrawal without utter destruction of mind and body. The higher forces which we contact on entering the Path cannot he played with, any more than you can play with fire. If we present ourselves to the Guardians of these powers as servants, it is against the law to release us from our pledge. Therefore the disciple used to he exhorted in olden times before taking his vow, and terrible ordeals were imposed upon him prior to his initiation.

Now turning to the other passage, "To cease from evil ways": Well, what is evil? And what are evil ways? There are many things which the man in the street would consider quite harmless, and yet to the disciple they are harmful. It is this difference that must be borne in mind. For the disciple to cease from evil ways means to refrain from every act (and thought is an act, let us well remember) which has not the absolute approval of the Higher Self. If the desire-nature and the mind have been so trained as to respond to every command of the Lord within, and if love has become the supreme Sovereign, ruling in the heart of the disciple, then may he pledge himself without fear of falling back, for then only can he be sure to have ceased from evil ways. There is a stage in the disciple's life which merits our special attention. It is the period of the great trial of his faith. At this stage the law of affinity makes itself felt. This well-known law which governs the mineral world holds good in the spiritual life of man. The affinities that bind atom to atom in the mineral world govern also the association of thoughts and ideas. If we try to cast aside the habits of a lifetime, as we generally do on entering the Path, then this law of affinity, which lies latent in our subconscious nature, suddenly rises against us and binds us to those tendencies which have grown up within us throughout the innumerable lives of the past. The disciple's task, having to face this opposition, is to fortify himself in his inner stronghold, and to exercise all the Divine patience of which he may be capable, in liberating himself by short degrees from the chains which he himself has forged. The quality most needful in this struggle is sweet patience. There may be failure to attain the ideal; usually there will be many failures, for even in the higher altitudes of spiritual endeavor there cannot be uninterrupted progress. You remember it is said, "Even Great Ones have fallen from the threshold." So there is great need for endurance and persistence, and after every slip and fall the disciple must rise and take heart and, as the Gita tells us, "return to the charge again and again."

Before the soul can stand in the Masters' presence this battle must have been fought and won. We are of no use to Them until this has been done.

To wash the soul's feet in the blood of the heart means to tear out the old remembrances root and branch, not only to be able to control desire but to have none; not only to look longingly to the great ideal before us, but to be earnestly engaged in its realization. The mystery of the threshold is to be ready; to have our loins girded and our lamps burning awaiting the pleasure of the King and His command. The soul, which has fitted herself in good time, will find that love's labor has not been lost and that a glorious fruition awaits her on the very threshold of the Temple. But even while preparing for it in this life, the truly-enlightened aspirant finds that it is indeed worth while to obey the vision he has seen, and the calmness and serenity which surrounds him after every conquest are the heralds of the great peace which shall enter his heart when the sublime end has been achieved and the day is at an end. Then the laborer shall find rest and while resting prepare the ground for his future career in cycles yet to come and in worlds yet to be.

We come now to a very important point, one which cannot be sufficiently emphasized, and that is the best ways and means to be adopted by the disciple to minimize the dangers of falling back after the Path has once been entered. There are many books instructing us in this and each of them is good in its own way. The Holy Qabalah teaches us that in most cases the career of incarnate man upon earth is first expiation and then the acquisition of new experience. Now as to expiation, the lives of many millions of human beings are really nothing more than one long chain of expiation. Think of those masses of toiling, sorrowing, starving people who have never had a chance in their lifetime. What are they here for? But even iii the case of those whose lives are along more pleasant lines, misery is not absent. There are plenty of heart-breaks and sorrows, the causes of which are not always evident to the sufferers. These causes lie generally far back in their former lives upon earth, this present incarnation having for its object the expiation of ancient wrongs. In the case of disciples, this truth of expiation should never be lost sight of, for it supplies a much needed explanation of many otherwise puzzling experiences that advanced students are called upon to endure.

Then there is the second object of incarnation, namely, the acquisition of new experience. This too applies to the disciple, for however detached from earthly things he may already be, he still may stand in need of some knowledge which can only be gained by his association with the children of men and by the observation of, and participation in, these manifold struggles and labors, incidental to earth-life. It is right here that he learns to be in the world but not of it.

Now before the soul can stand in the presence of the Masters, this ordeal of expiation and atonement must have been gone through. The blood of the heart in which the Soul's feet are to be washed is just this painful process of atoning for all the wrongs of days gone by. Thus the soul pays back the uttermost farthing, as all souls must do, and learns to identify herself with all that breathes and lives. No matter how humble and lowly a human creature may be, no matter how sinful and weak, the disciple who has learned his lessons aright knows all these creatures to be parts of the Great Divine Love to whom they are

just as dear as he himself. Thus the Qabalah tells us that by learning this last lesson of identification with high and low, the disciple becomes a cooperator with those high intelligences whom we call Masters, and, under Their guidance and with their help, he continues his career, ever upward, and ever onward, until he enters the presence of the Ancient of Ancients, the merciful Teacher of Gods, angels and men.

The secret Brotherhoods which formed the splendour of Egypt taught that life itself is the great Initiator, and the Qabalah, from which the Wisdom of the Egyptian Hierophants was derived, enjoined upon its students to "store the melody of life in their hearts" and to learn from it all that is needful.

IX.

THE LIGHT ETERNAL ACCORDING TO THE QABALAH

The Light Eternal comes from the bosom of God and shines in the eyes of every good man. It illuminates the face and lends a gentle touch to its expression and features. It is wholly absent in the countenance of the ungodly and no effort of theirs will imitate it. It is a gift from the good God to the children of light, and he bestows it upon them as a mark of his special affection.

Blessed be the man in whom this light has been lighted, for he will never lack anything needful, and even the wrath of his enemies will work goad for him. It is the light which the Prophets spoke of, and the Patriarchs desired so very much. It is the priceless pearl which it is well worth while to search after. Seek it, O Man! but not outside thee.

*For what is a seed but a cylinder on which is
registered in photographic script the
autobiography of its evolution.*

REGENERATION ACCORDING TO THE QABALAH

There is a beautiful passage in the Qabalah which explains the process of regeneration in nature. I cannot quote it verbatim, but it is to the effect that whenever any substance in Nature is to be renewed and regenerated, the negative or chemical force of light assumes the reins and increases the force of repulsion within the atom so that it subdues its opponent—attraction, and the atom is repelled and separated from its neighbour atoms.

When the positive or polar forces of light again asserts its power and increases the attraction, the atom acquires new affinities, and a new substance is formed. This happens to physical-plane atoms and to spiritual-plane ones as well. The thoughtful student will grasp the analogy between the two realms of nature and understand many things suggested so forcibly by this illustration.

Is it not the same with the individual soul when the time arrives for it to renew its substance and to be regenerated? Is not the passionate, impulsive nature, the lustful flesh, wishing to do the things that grieve the Spirit, the very principle of repulsion broken loose and overbalancing the attractive power of the spiritual atom?

What a lesson for us to be kind and patient and forgiving to those in whom sin and sense are still ruling! How it teaches us to see in those who have fallen only our younger brothers and sisters in whom a natural process is going on; yea, sometimes they may he our elders upon whom nature is just putting the finishing touch. As soon as the centripetal power of attraction again asserts itself in them, they may become the Helpers of their kind, Leaders and Benefactors of the race, using their experiences for the good of their unfortunate fellow-brothers and fellow-sisters.

A QABALISTIC PRAYER

Eternal God, Father of our spirit, enlighten us how to pray rightly unto thee. We would waste no vain words and we desire no material benefits. But our hearts yearn and long for the knowledge of Thee, and for Thy peace. In the fulness of Thy mercies grant us this prayer and fill our hearts with Thy love to overflowing so that we may not love only those who love us, but those who do not even know what love is. May we ever be aware of our humble origin and of our weakness in the days gone by, so that our hearts may open themselves not only to the strong who give us joy, but also to the weak ones who give us pain. It is hard for us to do it, hard indeed but enable us, O Heavenly Father, to sincerely try it and not to weary in the attempt. The road is steep, and dark is the night of our journey; our knees do often falter and we cannot as yet catch a glimpse of our eternal home, but we know that, even in the obscurity of the night, Thou art near. Unto Thee, then, we commend ourselves, and pray Thee to awaken and deepen within us the consciousness of thy presence so that we may go on our way rejoicing, until that day when our labors shall be over and we shall awaken in thy likeness.

Whatever the test that rends the soul,
Whatever the grief, that floods thy sorrowing heart with tears,
Whatever thy spirit fears,
Let it all lift thee up,
To kiss the very cross that blights thy life,
For in the fulness of His grace
Thou shalt see Him face to face,
And after the darkness of the night
Thou shalt rejoice in His glorious light.

www.ingramcontent.com/pod-product-compliance
Lightning Source LLC
Chambersburg PA
CBHW071750090426
42738CB00011B/2634